BIPOLAR
FROM THE
INSIDE

BIPOLAR
FROM THE
INSIDE

JUNE PIZANO

AuthorHouse™
1663 Liberty Drive
Bloomington, IN 47403
www.authorhouse.com
Phone: 1-800-839-8640

First published by AuthorHouse   08/30/2011

ISBN: 978-1-4634-2274-5 (sc)
ISBN: 978-1-4634-2273-8 (ebk)

Printed in the United States of America

This book is printed on acid-free paper.

CONTENTS

ACKNOWLEDGMENT

There are a few people in my life that have always been there for me in love and support.

My sister Ginger, who was my touch stone for my mood swings when I first started working with them.

Joni, my cousin, who has always been there in ways I can never repay. She is my Angel of Angels.

To Marilyn, my friend for editing the book for me, a million thanks.

To Rocio for all her help in preparing the cover, and the selections of the other Art. Thanks for making it happen. I owe you Champagne for life.

To my dearest friend, LA Doris (Sam), who through the years encouraged me to write Bipolar from the Inside. And was there to witness and see the changes that took place through the years, "always" making me aware of my progress with the illness, with support and acceptance.

To Shannon and Kelly, my beautiful daughters, for there love, that has helped me so much through the years. They are, by far, my best teachers.

And last, but not least, my husband Arturo who has taught me so much, and been able to love all of me. Thanks Mi Rey.

INTRODUCTION

Hi, my name is June Pizano.

The book I have written is to share my journey with the condition of being BIPOLAR.

I was diagnosed at 35 years old. From about 10 years old, I knew I was not like others. It was scary and fearful for me. No one seemed to understand what was wrong with me. My sleep was off; I had a bad temper, and little or no patience.

I had been talking to doctors for years. I was given tranquilizers, sleeping pills and mood elevators, and nothing helped. I was told to relax, to take a vacation, and to not stress, (but no one knew how to help me do that).

I attempted suicide for the first time at 12 years old, then again at 14, 17, 22, and 35. Perhaps there were more times, but there are years in which lot of things are mixed up as I was really manic. The suicides always followed the ending of a relationship. I had no self esteem. And because I received a lot of mental and physical abuse as a child, I was overly frightened about just about everything. If you have never experienced feeling suicidal, I do not know how to make you understand. I only know that when I was suicidal, I was helpless to help myself. When I came out of the depression, it was so difficult for me to understand how

I could think that way. But the fact is, I did, and those first 35 years were often horribly frightening, and no one was there to help. I am not blaming anyone anymore; I am just stating how it was.

At 35, I had a full manic episode. I ended up in a hospital on a 72-hour hold. It was at that time that I met the doctor that diagnosed me with the bipolar condition. He gave me some information to read and asked that I come back the next week and talk with him.

When I read the information, I was amazed to find out how much I could relate to it. It described my mood swings to a tee. I was not overjoyed to be BIPOLAR, however I was relieved to find out that it was not my imagination all those years, that indeed there was something wrong. There was a reason for my mood swings, and help for me. It validated what I HAD BEEN FEELING MOST OF MY LIFE.

I was prescribed lithium. It allowed me to slow down my thoughts enough to start to know what I could change and what I could not. It did not happen overnight, it took years. It was very hard to accept that if I did not take a pill I would be dysfunctional. There are so many days that I felt fine and thought I could do it alone. The fact is that I can not. This is part of being Bipolar. Part of the manic is when you think you can do anything and all things. It is so real when you are on a manic high, but, when you come down; it is as hard to believe some of your decisions as it were when you were on the depressive side and suicidal. It is a cunning condition. Stay as present with it as you can. Look for those red flags they are there. Remember, every time you go off the meds you are on a roller coaster ride for 3 to 6 weeks getting stabilized again.

It took me some time to accept that the meds were always necessary, especially when I was feeling better. Going off the medication always started a reaction of the manic side for me. And then the roller coaster would begin. I learned that it was an unwise decision to go off lithium. But it took some time to learn and my ego played havoc with me. When I was manic, my thinking was very bizarre, my reasoning was way off, and things that make perfect sense when I was on the high were way out of line when I was feeling better. I finally reached a point in my life where the ups and downs of the bipolar condition were taking their toll, and it was time to surrender and just do what was necessary. Again, it did not happen over night, as the manic side always resisted the meds. I had to be strong and really want to be a healthier and happier person.

The last 30 years have taught me a lot about the condition. I have learned through trial and error what I can and cannot do. I know now what does not work for me. I have been very blessed and have had wonderful doctors, friends and family helping me. It was not always easy, and still is not. But I have learned to say THANK YOU for all that is here for me.

The reason I wanted to write this book was to share the things I have learned, and found helpful, in hope that some or all of it can be helpful to you. It is one way I can give service and say thank you for all the help and blessings given me.

The writing of this book has been in the making for 34 years. I am delighted to have completed it on my 68th year.

These are the tools I have learned that help me.

1. CHECK IN PERSON
2. MORNING WRITTINGS
3. DIET

4. YOGA
5. MEDITATION
6. EXERSIZE
7. ALLOWING TIME
8. ORGANIZATION
9. COMMITMENTS
10. CHOICES
11. SLEEP
12. ART
13. BEING WITH NATURE
14. GIVING SERVICE

LEARNING ABOUT ME

I was a very frightened and lonely little girl. I learned to stuff my feeling at an early age. I think if there would have been help for my father, things would have been very different in our household. But help never came and the fear inside of me grew and grew. I do not know how much the abuse affected the Bipolar condition for me. By the age of 13 I wanted to be anywhere but my home. I had very little to do with my parents. In my mind they were dead to me. It was my way to survive.

Living in a world of fear as a child is paralyzing. Everything, and every person you encounter, is scary to you. This is partly due to the dysfunctional and bizarre way of thinking that is a symptom of being Bipolar.

As a young girl and woman relationships were destructive and difficult for me. My feeling that something was wrong with me made them very difficult. Still, even today, there are times when I have a hard time believing I am ok. Fortunately, now, I can come out of those feeling quickly. I am learning every year how to better work with the dysfunctional thinking. I can detach from things easily now. But as a small child it was hard. It was so painful, and scary.

I struggled with Bipolar symptoms all my life. At 35 I found out there was a name to go with what I had been feeling for years. It was a great relief for me. It gave me hope, and that is something I had had very little of my whole life.

I believe that we are our environment, so what I learned as a child, unfortunately carried through to how I interacted with my daughters. I did not behave to the same extreme as my dad, still it was not healthy. I had very little control over my mood swings. To finally get help and hope was the beginning of the healing and a healthier relationship with my girls. I am so thankful for that relationship today.

My daughters are so sweet, lovely, and smart and funny; they deserved so much more than they received from me. I am so blessed to still have them in my life. I believe that all things have a purpose. That belief has helped me with my guilt and sorrow over my earlier behavior.

I look up to my daughters and see so much strength in both of them. I would be lost without there kindness and support. Again, I feel very blessed that they are still in my life. There were times when they were not. I had a lot of amends to do. I had to learn to be responsible and patient and forgiving to my self and others. Writing this book and looking back into time, I can see how and where I have grown and I am grateful beyond words. I say 'Thank You' everyday.

Being Bipolar

Probably the most painful part of being Bipolar is the "incredible fear". It can be suffocating and paralyzing. It can be overwhelming and make decision-making very difficult. The simplest decisions like choosing whether you want a salad or potatoes for dinner can become a nightmare. Your busy mind is completely unable to hold onto just one thought. Your thinking is very scattered and confused. You lack patience of any kind and the impatience causes rudeness. Because of the impatience you have a short fuse, and you are ready for a fight. The anger and the rage become intensified easily. Your behavior can be very inappropriate. Your thinking is bizarre, and you become invincible. Then you start to become more delusional and then you begin to pace, more and more. Finally you can become suicidal.

All of my life I have lived with this horrible fear that something bad is going to happen. The fear is always there but it varies in intensity. I am not always aware of the fears when they start to become more intense. Through the years of working with the Bipolar I have learned to spot some red flags, one of those red flags is headache and nausea. When I was a young girl and woman I suffered from horrible migraines. It was the fear that caused the headaches. The fear that the mood swings will always be there. That I would always be disliked, that something bad is going to happen. I can now go for long periods of time without this intense fear, but it never completely leaves, and it clouds so many things. Every year I learn more how to detach from the fear, and recognize the red flags early on.

You have a cycle or a wave, or, simply put, mood swings. They can be very subtle and last a short time (a day or two), or they can be full blown, very extreme, and can last weeks or even months. When a cycle starts for me, it is like I am two people. The one inside my body is watching what the one outside my body is doing. During the first part of the cycle, the one on the inside is very much aware of what is happening. I am aware that I am being rude or very impatient or unreasonable, but I am helpless to stop the outside behavior. As the manic increases, I become less aware of my behavior. I do not see how bizarre my thinking and actions are becoming, and it continues to escalates until I crash. Then the depressive side of the cycle begins, and still I am unable to see how dysfunctional my behavior is. I loathe myself, cannot imagine anyone ever caring for me, and I become completely disgusted with me and my life. I wish I were dead. I think I should live alone and not have to inflict my misery on anyone else. Toward the end of the depression, I am able to be aware of my behavior and know the depression will end, and then it does. The effects of the cycles play a toll on my body, mind and spirit. It is hard to understand how I can behave in certain ways, but it happens and, if I am doing "my work" with the bipolar condition it is and has become more and more workable through the years. But I must do "the work". For me that is my check in person, diet, exercise, yoga, meditation, morning writings, organization, allowing extra time, being with nature, art, commitments, choices, giving service, making space, sleeping well etc. The cycles still appear today, but they are less intense and do not last as long. The work is what this book is about. Do the work, your life can and will be more functional. Say thank you for being able to do the work, and have a healthier and happy life style.

My work every day goes like this: I wake and do morning writing (that helps me to see where I am in the cycle or, if I am not in a cycle; it helps me to know how I am feeling. I wait to read my morning writings at the end of the week. That way I almost always see a pattern. My writing might be talking about wanting to slow down or sleep better, etc). Next I do yoga and meditation yoga (yoga and meditation always calms me down and makes me smile). Then I organize my day, (organization helps the busy mind). If things are in order and I allow a little extra time, I am less scattered and confused. That helps the Manic a lot. I eat a healthy breakfast,(I like to start with oatmeal and fruit. I avoid mixing my proteins and carbohydrates. I stay away from sugar. I eat a lot of green leafy veggies). Somewhere in my day I take a strong swim, or walk. (This helps with my extra energy, frustrations and my impatience's). I do my meditation and, in the latter part of the day I do some type of art. (Art relaxes me and the colors I choose give me a good insight to my moods).

I was really pleased when I finally made the commitment to write the book, however I was not prepared for the pain that it stirred up and the intensity of that pain. I started having migraines again and felt like a failure. I did not like myself. For years now I have functioned so well that I had forgotten what it was like to feel the intensity of the disease. The mood swing I experienced took me by surprise. It was full blown before I realized it. I had to start to limit the time I spent on the book. I had to stop writing for awhile, and take strong walks and swim. It is times like that, that make me appreciate all the things I have learned to help myself. I did a lot of yoga, meditation and stayed away from all sugars. I knew I would feel better, I knew it would pass, and I also knew it would return again, and again. As long as I do my work I will survive it. The illness is very confusing. If you are going to be functional you cannot live like everyone else. Your diet has to be healthy. You need to stay as present as possible. That can be difficult when the fear hits you and you want to run away from everything. But you must be strong and do what work works for you to stay functional.

I have tried to explain this disease to many people through the years, and people just do not get it. My most common reaction is that I could change my behavior if I really wanted to. I try to be as clear as possible about what is going on, but people really do not care. It does not make them bad or insensitive; it just means they do not get what kind of pain you are in. Anybody that is Bipolar has experienced this I am sure. It makes it so hurtful sometimes, but it is what it is.

I experience cycles with Bipolar and, often I can catch a cycle before it starts, but even now I do not always catch it. I did not catch this last cycle until I was half way through it.

What happens for me in a cycle is first off I start to become more hyper, I can not sit still, I pace a lot. I become increasingly more impatient and then manic. When I am in the first part of the manic I feel great. I feel invincible. I think I can accomplish anything and I can. Then the manic becomes fiercer and I lose my patience's with just about everything. My mind becomes speeded. My thoughts are cluttered. I become very scattered. I can no longer hold on to just one thought. The more scattered the more the fear starts in and by now everything starts to overwhelm me. Simple decisions become increasingly more difficult. I have incredible fear that something bad is going to happen. The more manic I become the more suffocating the fear. I stop sleeping through the nights for days, or weeks sometimes and then the down side appears. Nothing matters, or pleases me. I have difficulty being positive about anything.

The cycle can be triggered by lack of sleep, a lot of stress, primal fears, etc. Mine just got triggered from the primal fears that are coming up with the writing of the book.

Last week I felt very low, very depressed, felt like a failure. I felt that no one cared. I had trouble sleeping. I could not stop crying I felt sorry for me, and then mad at me for not being stronger. At times like these it is important to embrace the disease. Embrace the pain and the sorrow. It is so important to embrace all of you now.

Remember when the confusion is there it triggers the fear, and the fear triggers the manic.

Make a point to be with positive people. Eat well, get plenty of rest. Meditate, do yoga. There are many things that you can do to help you. You're worth it.

I feel so thankful and blessed that I have found so many things that help me to be a stronger, healthier person. If the ones I talk about are not all for you, there will be other things. As long as you work on being present with the condition, there is help for you. I CAN PROMISE YOU THAT.

Transition Into Meds

When I was diagnosed with the disease Bipolar, lithium was the most commonly used drug. There are many other medications out today and you need to talk to your doctor about them. There might be a better drug suited for you. I have chosen to stay on lithium because it works better than others for me, and it works well. It took some time and doing to decide to stay on the lithium. It is funny how the mind works, how we feel it is wrong to have to take something to feel better. There is a crazy guilt involved. Even with something as simple as taking aspirin for a headache, we think somehow that there is no need for it.

I was resentful of having to take lithium at the beginning and resisted it on and off for some time. As soon as I would start to feel better, I would think I was ok and did not need to take the lithium any longer. I would go off the drug thinking I did not need it, only to find out, once again I did. The stress of going on and off was very harmful to my body and mind. It would take weeks and sometimes months to stabilize on the drug again.

My experience with lithium, and needing to take the drug took me years to really accept and understand the need for it and how it worked. It also took years not to feel guilty or think that I had done something wrong to be on lithium—to think there was something more I could do to not have to stay on the lithium. I finally came to accept my body needed the drug. I do not understand why and I no longer care. I have come to be very thankful for the drug and how it has helped me. Going on and off lithium took its toll on me.

When I first went on lithium I did not really notice any change. However others did. They found me much easier to be with. They found me much calmer. I started taking much more responsibility for what I did and said. My reasoning was much clearer. Before lithium I never took responsibility for my actions. It was always someone or something else that caused what happened. My reasoning was very bizarre back then. I am sure at times my thinking is still bizarre—the difference is that I know it now and have learned ways to think more functional.

I reason better today than ever before. Making decisions no longer frightens me. There was a time when the simplest decision would set off an anxiety attack, so severe it was suffocating.

Changes do not happen overnight, but through the years you will notice subtle changes. Be grateful for the changes you experience.

There are times when one of my daughters will recall something I did, and I am shocked with how poorly I handled the situation. There are many things I did back in my 30s that today I would never consider doing. So many things years ago were dealt with in a very hurtful way. Before lithium, and for years after first taking the medication, I still dealt with things in a negative and hurtful way. It takes what it takes to change the things we need to, but things change not all at once, but they change.

My life is so much better with the medication I am much calmer. My stress level is much less. My patience has improved a lot (however my work with my patience is by far the hardest part for Me.), my fears are all helped by the meds.

I have been told by doctors that only about 30% of people that take lithium are helped like I am. I feel very fortunate for how well it works for me. I say "thank you" all the time. However, there are a lot of newer drugs out now. It is important to find the one that works best for you, and it could take going on and off some drugs to find the best one for you. Once again you need to talk to your doctor about this.

If you ever decide to go off your medication, make sure you do it with the help of your doctor. It can be very dangerous to do it on your own.

Lithium is only a part of the recovery, and I cannot stress that enough. It is imperative that you become very present with all your actions. Often people want to just take a pill and not do the work that is required to go with the pill. Lithium allowed me to see what other responsibilities I needed to work on in my life. It allowed me to see what needed my attention and what did not.

Once you accept that you need the medication. The real work begins.

Taking a medication is just taking a medication. Why my body does not manufacture salt I do not know. What I do know now is it does not make me a bad person, because I need medication. It is a wise person that does what needs to be done. The work is there for you. The rewards are a strong and healthy body, mind and spirit.

Embrace everything about bipolar. It will really help the healing. Be thankful for the medication. It is important to be thankful for the help the medication allows you and not get hung up on not being able to do it on your own.

To be able to sleep better, to have more patience, to feel less angry—to have happiness and joy back in your life, to feel less scattered—these are the positive things to focus on and be THANKFUL for the medication. And embrace it.

Lithium

When I was diagnosed with bipolar lithium was the most commonly used drug. There are many others out today.

Lithium works well for about 30% of the people that take it . . . I am one of those people and very grateful that it works so well.

There might be a newer drug better suited for you.

I have chosen to stay on it because it works better than other medicines did and it works well.

You need to speak with your doctor about this.

Lithium made it possible for me to slow down my mind enough to know what I am capable of changing and what I am not capable of changing.

It allowed me to take steps necessary, to be a more functional and a much happier person.

I was resentful of having to take lithium at the beginning and resisted it off and on for a few months. As soon as I would be feeling well I would think I was ok and did not need to take it any longer.

When I went off the drug thinking I did not need it, only to find out once again, that I really did, the going off and on was very stressful to my body. It can take weeks to stabilize again.

It is very important to embrace the illness, and be thankful for the medication. It is important to be thankful for the help the medication allows and not to get hung up on not being able to do it on your own.

To be able to sleep, have more patience, to feel less anxious, happier, less scattered, these are the things to focus on and be thankful for the drug. Embrace it.

Embrace The Disease.

It is very important to embrace the disease, even the parts you dislike, or perhaps hate.

When you are first diagnosed, you are torn between being happy to finally know what is happening to you, and the feeling that if you really tried harder you would be ok without medication. It is a Catch 22. No one wants to believe that they need to take something to be functional. There is a lot of guilt-here. However, if you can look at that pill as something wonderful for you, something that enables you to have a happy more peaceful life, something that allows you to have loving and kind relationships with those you love, then that pill becomes your savior and you are so pleased to have found it. I am very happy to have lithium and that I am one of the 30% it works well for. I say thank you everyday.

One of the things I have learned, which is a great gift of the disease, is that the manic state, at a low dose, keeps you happy and positive. I learn quickly, I am not frightened by new careers-moving to a new state or country has always been easy for me. I have always enjoyed meeting new people.

It is important to accept all states of being bipolar, not just the high side. It is important to accept the anger, the hate, the impatience, the fear, the sadness, the pain, the rage, the self-loathing, and the negative self talk.

Here is where healthy choices can really pay off. Make it a point to be more responsible for your choices in food, sleep, exercises, friends etc.

You have a choice with anger. You can embrace it or fuel it. There is almost always certain emotion and things that trigger anger. Learn what your red flags are and work with them. If you have difficulty figuring out what triggers you, go talk to a professional and learn what it is you need to do. It took me years to realize that I did not have to fight anymore. With the help of good doctors, family and friends I learned how to work with my anger. During my first visit to a psychiatrist, the doctor asked me what I was so angry at. I was so shocked that he saw the anger in me. During that session, I learned how much anger I had for my father. I was in disbelief. It is very confusing when you hate a parent. There is so much guilt for feeling that way. Learning to understand all that was a gift. It gave me something to work with. I started realizing there was hope out there for me. Growing up in a physically and mentally abusive home taught me a lot of dysfunctional ways of dealing with things and people. It is our jobs as adults to clear up these patterns and learn positive choices in all things. For years I really believed I had to fight for everything. I do not, and neither do you. I would stay in an argument, and then I would become very angry. I make the choice today to walk away from an argument. It is amazing how that can help balance you. A short walk around the block can really clear the head, and even put a smile on your face.

If you choose to hate, you block the love. The hate we carry hurts us. It plays hell on our liver so learn to embrace it. It is so important to let go of that hate. When you are feeling hate, choose to change that to compassion. I worked on compassion with my father who I thought I hated for years. The beauty of that work has freed me from that painful emotion to a healthier one of compassion. It freed my soul. It feels so good to think of my father without anymore pain, sadness, hate or anger. Embrace those feelings; they are there for a reason.

If you are an impatient, person it is probably more important for you to make sure you sleep well, watch your diet for too many stimulants, and to exercise. Watch your impatience, and learn from it. Become very present with your moods. The more you take care of your impatience the happier you are. If you make that effort, one day you will see the results. It takes time, but we are worth it.

When you feel, fear is almost always fueled by some type of confusion. Keep things as simple as you can to avoid any undue confusion. Take that extra fifteen minutes of time; it can really help that fear to not escalate. It is important to have a safe place where you can go that gives you the space you need to deal with the fear. When it becomes suffocating, it is a good time to make the choice to work with your breathing. Practicing breathing can help the fear beyond belief. All of these things are a way to embrace your disease. It is important to love all of you to stay happy and functional.

Sadness can be so overwhelming. It is important to identify what is making you sad. It has to be dealt with. It will not help if you ignore it or get mad at yourself because of it. Sadness can be gone in a few hours or days. But it will be gone. Knowing that helps me when I am really sad, I just keep reaffirming that it wont be around long. Sadness triggers the pain, again, embrace it and give it the attention it needs. It is not a bad thing, it just is an emotion and it will go away. It is important to feel the pain, but once you have felt it let it go. It no longer serves a purpose.

Rage is all those things you "stuff". Eventually, if you stuff your feeling all the time, there will be an explosion, so it is extremely important to find different releases for them. Swimming or biking is a great outlet for me. But the most important part is learning to work with the rage-learning to express our feeling calmly and know it is acceptable to do this and it is your right as a human being. You might have to work with a doctor if your rage is out of hand. When you learn to express yourself calmly, the rage will lessen and lessen. But the most important part about rage is to not stuff those feeling. It is ok to feel. Rage can take its toll. It uses a lot of energy and it is so hard on the liver.

My self-loathing is from the part of me that does not want to get better. It is a confusing feeling. However, when I find myself doing things that are dangerous for me and not stopping, I know I need to get back into a strict diet and to take more responsibility for my actions. When I am being responsible and taking good care of my eating habits, I have no self-loathing. And, it is my responsibility to look at what got me off track and to deal with it and not stuff it. I can choose not to do the things that get me off track. I can also make the choice to like and love me.

My negative self-talk is horrible. If anyone else talked to me the way I do I would never speak to them again. My early life left a lot of scars but I am happier today than ever before, and I laugh a lot at myself for the things I think. Laughter helps. I have a negative track that goes daily. For instance, I am always too fat, (I know I am not fat, but the tape goes). One day I think I am looking pretty good, and the next I cannot stand myself. The better I take care of myself, the less negative the self talk. I work with staying focused on all the positive things I do. When I am working on this, I actually start to like me. How great that feels. So, for every negative thought, reach for two positive ones. It works—I promise.

It is important to look at the lessons in the illness, and all that you are learning about yourself and the disease. It is important to know that your whole self is ok. The bipolar condition is just a part of who you are.

If I focus on the bad things, I can become very sad. However if I look at the whole, there are always great things to see. We need to see them, or we feel that no one will like us, or cares.

I have great anger; I also have a great sense of humor. I have hate for some things, but I also have a great capacity to love. The negative self-talk can get in my way, but if I catch it and just stop it, I am ok. It is finding your balance, and once the balance is in place, good things come. They just do.

Know that there are great lessons to be learned.

Every year I learn many new things. Every year I marvel at how my consciousness, my compassion, and my lack judgment have grown. Look for the lessons; notice what you understand this year differently than before. Get involved on your journey—the more involvement the healthier the journey. Thank yourself often, for all you do. You deserve it.

Know that you are able to be functional, and a happy being. Functional behavior does not happen overnight. The more disciplined you are the happier you will be. It is our work, no one else's.

Look for the blessings in the disease they are there I promise.

You. It's been to
long already since
I've played with
you
    Will See you Marron

Space + More Space

Doctors And Others

I was told by many doctors in my early years that I was fine, just stressed. I knew better, but until I was in my 30s there was never a doctor that had any idea I was Bipolar.

Maybe I needed to be stronger with the doctors I talked with, I am not sure. What I do know is that my life before I found out about the disease was dysfunctional, and I was very unhappy and often suicidal.

Doctors and others do not always know what is good or right for you. They are not experiencing what you are and most probably never will. I have been blessed to have worked with many wonderful doctors. But in my teens up, and until I was 34, any doctor I talked to had no idea how to help me. Doctors and others do not always have the answers. As a young teenager and woman it was very frustrating for me. I slept poorly all the time, and had little or no control of my temper, let alone mood swings. People thought I was just very uptight and intense. I was very hard to talk to when I was manic; and flew off the handle over the smallest of thing. My beautiful daughters suffered the most. It breaks my heart to think of some of my actions and the effect the Bipolar had on them. No one in my family ever talked about my moods except to whisper behind my back and asks "how is June today". Until I was diagnosed at

35, I had no idea what was going on with me. I did think I was a little crazy, and that was scary and frightened the hell out of me.

Start to explore yourself. Learn your body rhythms. Get in touch with your inner voice.

1. Art
2. Morning Writings
3. Meditation
4. Yoga
5. Etc.

Everyday create space for you and ask yourself how you feel and wait for the answer. Be as present as you can be with yourself. Had I tried to check in more with my feeling and body rhythms, maybe I could have given a doctor better information on how I was feeling. The more we know about ourselves, the more present we are and the more you can help a doctor help you. No one knows your body or your mind better than you. If you have never worked with a doctor, or have never found a doctor that works well with you, keep trying to find the right doctor for you. They are there. Don't let a doctor intimidate you. Ask as many questions as you can. A good doctor will welcome your questions. If you react differently to a treatment or medication than you were told, question it. Question the doctors, until you get the results you are seeking. It could take going to several different doctors. When you find the right one, you will know, and the right one can help you a great deal.

THERPY

Find a physiatrist you work well with. You do not have to like them, for them to help. The first physiatrist I worked with I disliked a lot at the beginning. That changed after a few visits and I started learning a lot about myself and why I did some of the things I did. It is a slow process, but a must. Sometimes it is hard to see our pattern and to know how to change them, that is where a good physiatrist comes in. If you do not resist the help it goes so much faster, but that can be tricky because of our egos, and the bizarre ways you view things being Bipolar.

I have worked with several therapists and learned a great deal from them.

The first one put me in touch with my anger and rage. Up until that time I did not even realize who I was angry with. I just knew I had a lot of anger in me.

My anger and rage were so intense I used to scare people. I would get so angry and with the rage I was totally out of control. Being that angry and full of rage for me means I am overwhelmed with fear. I am terrified and I am Manic as hell. The therapist helped me understand this part of me and gave me many tools to help me work with the fear, but before I was diagnosed with Bipolar I had no idea what was happening to me or why. I was so out of control. I had no idea at that time how much confusion could trigger the manic.

The first physiatrist told me to carry a bag around with me and cover my face when I got mad. He said my facial expression were like a ghoul. I thought that was funny at that time. My thinking in those days was very bizarre, and dysfunctional.

So, the 1st psychiatrist put me in touch with my anger. I learned all my rage and anger were from the fear I felt. The fear I felt in my body is often overwhelming. I have learned through the years and different Therapies what I need to do to defuse the fear. I now can work fairly easily with that fear.

The 2nd psychiatrist is a brilliant doctor I met here in Mexico.

At the time I met her she used Crystal Therapy. We worked a lot on a primal issue, and had good results. I was able to detach from some childhood traumas. And that lessened the fears a lot.

My father was Bipolar, and had severe mood swings. I was in and out of hospitals from his abuse until I was 12 years old. By 12 years old I had decided that no one would ever hit me again. The abuse did not cause the Bipolar, however I am sure it had a negative effect for me. I have known many Bipolar people that did not have abusive parents, but they are Bipolar.

The guilt I felt for the hate I had for my father was unbelievable. Through different therapies I no longer feel that hate for my father; I feel only compassion for him now. And feeling compassion is so much better than caring around that hate.

My 2nd psychiatrist had me stair at a picture of my father for an hour at a time. I was told to see what I could see. What I saw was this very sad man. I could not find a picture of my father where he was smiling. The practice opened my heart to compassion. After I was then able to spend a few days on a visit with my father, instead of a few minutes. My father was never treated for the Bipolar, what a shame.

If there is someone you carry a lot of hate for, try the picture. Remember when you are experiencing hating someone, you are harming your liver, your well being and most of all you are closing your heart to love.

The third physiatrist I worked with I did some very strong Primal work. I did regression work and that really opened my eyes to why I carried so much fear in my being . . . I started understanding more and more what caused my Bipolar and emotional problems and I started to see the light at the end of the tunnel.

In Primal work I learned that all my aches and pains were a part of me that I had ignored, and stuffed way down inside of me. I have learned to open to these pains and deal with them. I now take more responsibility for my life. I could not have done without the help of theses doctors and friends.

I have learned to enjoy the philosophy of Buddhism, and it has helped a lot with taking responsibility for my life.

I am out of the blaming others for why I am the way I am. I have learned to take full responsibly for my life and it feels great.

I am happy and so thankful to have my fears under control and lead a functional and happy life. I am also so grateful to have a better understanding of the Bipolar. Learning to accept that I am Bipolar and that it is a daily challenge for me to work with the disease has changed my life . . . The rewards have been great. To sit and write a book is something I never could have accomplished years ago. To be able to calm my mind is a true Blessing, I am forever thankful for that and being able to work with the bipolar as well as I do.

SUICIDES

My first suicide attempt was when I was 12 years old. I drank a bottle of coke with aspirins. Nothing happened. Because of all the physical abuse in my family, I had no self esteem. I was constantly overwhelmed with fear. I desperately wanted to feel loved and I did not. I felt no self worth; I felt like something was horribly wrong with me. To believe you are a bad person—a bitch—day in and day out is horrible. I was told all of those things daily. My salvation at 12 was a 15 year old boy I used to swim with. Our parents broke us up because we were too young. It broke my heart I wanted to die. I felt that there was no one there for me. And I believed that. That was the trigger for my first suicide attempt.

When you're more manic than depressive, (I am), your highs often keep you away from the suicidal part of the disease. But when the crash comes—and it always does—you are lost and overwhelmed with fear. You just want to die. There is no light at the end of the tunnel, or so you think. I am sorry no one knew how to help me until I was 35. If I would have found lithium by my teens, my whole world would have been different.

If you have never thought of suicide you probably won't get this. But it is real, and it is scarier than hell.

No one in my family ever talked about my suicides. No one ever took me to a doctor. No one cared. Or maybe the truth is that it frightened everyone and no one knew what to do.

But the reality is thinking suicidal is a horrible experience.

I have been writing this book nine months and this is by far the most difficult part to address. I have had so many years now without suicidal thoughts that I am finding it hard to reach back to those times. I feel so blessed that part of the illness is over for me. There was a time I never believed it possible.

My second suicide attempt occurred when I was 14. It was triggered by a broken relationship, and it destroyed me. I slit my wrist with a razor blade and my brother found me and told me if I ever did that again he would have me locked up. He had a nurse friend of his bandage my wrists, and that was that. Nothing more was said about what I had done. My fear was that he would put me in a mental institution. There was so much abuse at my home, that an outside relationship was what I poured myself into. My relationship became my reason to live. I had no idea what a pretty and smart person I was. It took till my 30s to start seeing my self worth.

At 17, I tried to end my life again, I felt I would never be able to have a healthy relationship and knew something was out of balance for me. My friends were supportive, but they were lost as to what could help me.

At 22, I had just had my first daughter, and I slit my wrist when she was 6 weeks old. I had been on a manic high for over 3 months. Nobody said anything. My husband pretended it did not happen. No one wanted to talk about it. I was so frightened. I think that having the baby caused my hormones to be off and—coupled with the manic—it was one of the scariest times of my life. I thought I was going crazy more than once. Trying to kill myself after just having a new baby was crazy.

I was divorced when my girls were 2 and 5 years old. I then went into a deep depression for over a year. Everyone was fed up with me. They thought I could do better if I wanted.

I talked to many doctors. They prescribed tranquilizers, and they depressed me even more. It was a horrible time for my daughters in those years. I do not have a clear memory for about ten years. In my 30s, I got my real estate license and did extremely well.

I was excited about being able to buy a nice house and car, and cloths for the girls and me. I bought a lot of property, which would have provided for my daughters education. But I was working way too hard, with too many hours, and the manic continued to grow and, because my thinking was so bizarre and dysfunctional, I had a manic episode and ended up in a hospital. Still very manic, even with medication, I continued to work too hard and eventually I lost everything I had been working so hard for. Thank God that was my last time going that low into depression. Things started to get better then with the medication and the therapy, and a year or so later the horrible depressions and suicidal thoughts were gone.

Things can and do get better. I am happy to say I am living proof of that.

CHECK IN PERSON

When you first find out that you are Bipolar, one of the most important things you will learn to do is to be as "present" as you can be. It is important in the beginning to take a look at how the illness works in your particular case as you begin to rebuild your life and be more functional. At this stage it is really important to have a person you trust completely working with you, and pointing out things you might miss. I call this person a "check in person". It is like starting kindergarten and working your way up through the years to graduation. The check-in person is very helpful in the first few years. After the first few years, I was aware enough of my own situation to work with my illness on my own.

When you are Bipolar, there is a cycle that the illness runs. The cycle is your mood swings. The mood swings are like a wave with the ups and downs.

If you can catch the cycle or the wave, on the onset, it does not always have to run the full cycle, or be as severe. A full cycle for me is going from being slightly manic to full-blown manic and then going down fast to the depression. It can be very scary when you become so manic you cannot sleep or eat, and equally scary when you get to the depressive side and feel suicidal. It can be difficult to catch even with someone helping you. I am fifty years into the illness and I still sometimes find myself on the roller coaster unable to stop it. That is why yoga, meditation, morning writings, diet (really watching the sugar intake) etc. are important to do all the time. Since I have changed my life to a healthy life style, it is very rare for me to have a severe mood swing. The better I take care of myself, the better handle I have on the "wave." Having a check-in person, is very helpful for keeping you "present". Staying present allows a better chance of catching the cycle. It is very important to be aware of your patterns. When you have a check-in person, they will hear in your voice if you are becoming more manic or depressed. There are times your check-in person will be aware that the cycle has begun before you are. That is why it is very important to trust your check-in person completely and know that he or she is being honest with you.

I used my sister Ginger, as a check-in person, for about two years after I was diagnosed.

She would tell me if I sounded depressed or really hyper. She might ask me questions about my diet or if I had been sleeping well or if I had been exercising. She helped keep me on track.

The questions Ginger asked me would help her to help me know if a cycle was starting. The cycles can be very sneaky. A check-in person once a day or week is very important at the beginning of learning to work with the bipolar condition.

In the beginning, I was often taken by surprise that a cycle had already started.

It is much easier today.

The cycle varies from person to person. My cycle goes like this.

1. I become very happy.
2. There is nothing that I do not think I could do, or do well.
3. I have endless energy.
4. I want to do a lot of things with friends.
5. I sleep less and less.
6. My impatience becomes stronger and stronger.
7. My mind goes at warp speed.
8. I begin to think something is wrong with me.
9. I think I am unlikable.
10. The anger and rage begins, and takes hold of everything in my path.(the mania is in full force now)
11. I become abusive, condescending, and completely unreasonable.
12. My thinking becomes very bizarre.
13. I cannot sleep, or eat.
14. Now the down side begins all I want to do is sleep.
15. I am frightened of all things.
16. Everything overwhelms me.
17. I become very depressed.
18. I have suicidal thoughts.
19. LACK OF SELF-ESTEEM.

And then I am ok again (functional). My cycles are not that severe now. I am never suicidal anymore. I am now able to track the mood swings much better. When I first start becoming manic and feel so happy—that I could do anything—I know to stop and check to determine if I have had too much sugar, if I need to do more yoga, if I need to take a strong swim, etc. If I haven't been sleeping well, I know I need more space, more quiet time.

So, once again, it is important to watch your patterns. That is where morning writing can help you. If you write every morning for ten minutes, you will see a pattern. You will also see when the pattern starts to change. My writing actually is very different when I am manic.

My check-in person was so important at the beginning in helping me become more functional. I was very fortunate to have my sister help me. It is a very sensitive subject when someone tells you you're off. So, again, make sure it is someone you can trust completely and who you will not get angry with when they are trying to help you. I am sure it was not the easiest thing for my sister to do because of the sensitivity evolved. I do know that because of her help I became healthier sooner. Once I understood the mood swings, I was able to monitor myself. The medication also helped in slowing down my mind so I could be more focused. Find that person you trust and start working with them. Make you life happier and more functional.

Morning Writings

My mind seems to never stop. When too many things are going on at once, I become very confused and that brings on the fear and the manic. I find if I write for ten minutes when I first wake up every morning, it helps to slow down my busy mind. I am more settled and ready to begin the day. The morning writings seems to empty out both my conscious and unconscious mind, and it helps me to quiet my mind.

I do not read what I have written every day. I wait a week to read the pages, and then I can see a pattern. This helps me to keep myself in check. To stay more present . . .

I might see a pattern of wanting to slow down. That is a red flag as I realize I maybe becoming more Manic. I might see a need to be more positive. That is a red flag that I am becoming more on the depressive side and perhaps need to check my diet more closely. If I write that I am feeling unloved; I am probably in a depression. If I write that I am not sleeping, I am Manic and probably have another cycle started. The more aware you are with your feelings, the easier it is to have better control over what is going on with the ups and downs of the disease.

The less you can control what you write, the better. The goal is to get as much garbage out of your thinking mind so that you can slow down a bit.

A few pages of writing a day can keep you more present with the bipolar condition. The more present you are the easier the cycle. The easier the cycle, the happier and calmer you are.

Diet

I tried to kill myself about two years after I started taking lithium. I was in deep, deep, depression. I was at a loss of what I needed to do, and made the decision to work on my diet. My cousin Joni had a health food store and was very knowledgeable in nutrition. She suggested going off all sugar, and doing a colon and liver detoxifying program. We worked together for over a year. After that time, I slowly started reintroducing things in my diet. I continued to work with another nutritionist for another year. I went back on sugar slowly, and learned what my body could handle, and what it could not and what I can and cannot do diet-wise. I am attuned to my body and my body needs now. Through the years, I have worked with different nutritionists and doctors, and have fasted to keep my body fine-tuned. Watching my sugar intake has made a huge difference in my manic side, and the depression side. We have all heard of the sugar blues.

It is important to read labels and see if sugar has been added. You will probably be amazed at the amount that is put in so many things. Grapes, raisins, oranges, bananas are all high in sugar. Fruits are important, so go for green apples, or cranberries. Find out what works for you. Besides fruits, watch the breads, wine, alcohol, cakes, candies, ice cream etc. Bread an alcohol turn to sugar and speeds up the manic mood for me. When I went off sugars for one year, and was amazed at the difference in my mood swings. I felt happier and much stronger.

The 2nd nutritionist taught me how to eat a healthy way for my body, which for me is watching my sugar intake and eating lots of green leafy veggies. Veggies are my friend. I eat lots of green leafy veggies. I try to have 70% veggies with my meals. Be careful with carrots, lots of sugar. The veggies give us our nutrients and vitamins, which help keep us calmer, naturally.

I was also taught more about detoxifying. Because I carry a lot of rage and anger in my body, it affects my liver, so it is important for me to do regular liver flushes. I use a tablespoon of olive oil with a clove of garlic smashed in it. I do this three times a month or three times a week depending on my body needs and stress level.

Find a good nutritionist and work closely with that person to know your body better. The stress level in my body is normally higher than most people because of the Bipolar, so it is necessary, to address the stress and work with it daily. Find a good person to work with and learn what will and what will not work for you.

At the beginning of eating healthier, I felt deprived by not getting to have a brownie or ice cream anytime I wanted. However, not long after I started eating healthier, I began to feel so much better that I became grateful for what I had learned and no longer had felt deprived of anything—just thankful for being happier. I am now so grateful for all I have been taught and the way it makes me feel. I so often hear in conversations that diet is not that important. It is, especially if you are Bipolar. I have not thought about or tried to commit suicide since my diet became healthy. That says it all for me. Too much sugar is poison for me. It is great not to go so low that you want to die. If you have never had suicidal thoughts, you probably will not understand completely. But those of you that do understand, I hope you will work with your diet. Good Luck, you have nothing to lose by trying it, and so much to gain.

Yoga

When you are bipolar, and your mind is going 100 miles a minute, you get to the point where you would do just about anything to slow yourself down. Breathing is one of the best natural ways to do that. Also when you are bipolar, you often sleep poorly. That, coupled with the fast-paced mind, can wear you out, and anyone else that is around you! It is very hard on the body, when your stress level is very high, and you have little or no patience.

I started a yoga practice before I was prescribed lithium. I was desperately looking for something that would help me to calm down because at this time in my life I was very manic all the time. I made very bad decisions and I had a bizarre way of viewing things. I did not sleep well. I had no patience.

My mood swings were very severe. I was very hard to be around. I believe I scared a lot of people at that time of my life. That's why I was searching for something that would help me to be more functional, and calmer. I wanted something "natural".

Thanks to God, I found yoga.

I could not sit still for more than a minute before yoga, and today I can meditate for an hour and love it.

I began to teach yoga almost 20 years ago. I was 50 years old. It was—and still is—the best job I have ever had. I excelled in it and loved it. And, giving service by helping other people through yoga is the best. Yoga means balance, the balance of mind, body and spirit.

Yoga truly helped save my life. It is by far one of the best things I have done for me. I am at my best when I do yoga. Yoga gets me in-touch with my breathing. My breathing work helps slow my fast paced mind down naturally. It helps me sleep better, and helps me with my impatience.

It helps me stay centered. Helps work out the negativity I hold in my body. I work with my 'charkas" with my practice. It is a great way to release what no longer serves as purpose in my life. I do yoga six days a week for 50 minutes, sometimes longer.

I have been blessed living in an area of Mexico where some of the best yogis come to do workshops. While teaching at a beautiful retreat center in Mexico I was fortunate, to attend class with the best.

There are so many wonderful things in our life that take us by surprise. Yoga was one of those things for me.

The more we can do to learn how to read our body, mind and spirit, the easier the bipolar becomes.

My suggestion to you is to find a yoga teacher that "resonates" with your body. It might take a few classes, but you can find the right one.

Meditation

My first experience with meditation was almost painful for me, because, in "my early days" dealing with my bipolar condition, I would have an anxiety attack if I had to sit still for even a minute. I did not have any tools yet to slow down my mind which, in those days, was like a fast train out of control.

I always had at least ten things going on in my mind at the same time that caused a lot of confusion, and confusion always triggered the fear. The fear of something bad about to happen. And then I would become manic.

It has taken years of practice, and not giving up, for me to master meditation. All of the practice, and more practice, has been well worth the end results. At one time in my life I had no idea I could ever master meditation.

Let alone sitting still. It took a lot of discipline, but watching the changes come through the years has been a fabulous reward for all that discipline. To lie or sit still for an hour and empty my thinking mind completely is a blessing. It helps me rejuvenate and makes my life so much more peaceful and enjoyable. To be able to experience the bliss of a quiet mind is something I do not think most bipolar people can relate too.

Like yoga, meditation has saved my life by allowing me to slow down just a bit. It helps me to think more functional and centered. It calms me down.

There are so many types of meditation, and it is so personal that it can take some trial and error to find what is best for you. And like so many things, we are constantly changing our needs. So what works at one stage of our life may evolve to something else at another stage.

I practiced with pranayama yoga. I enjoy the different breaths with it. I enjoy the way the breaths are broken down. I have found great inner peace with the practice of meditation.

When the stillness comes it is like going home deep inside me where I know that everything is going to be alright and safe. For someone bipolar having that feeling might be as foreign to you as going to the moon.

Pranayama is a must for me. It is therapeutic and the breath is magical.

Pranayama

1. Calms you
2. Releases tension
3. Relaxes the mind

What works for me is ten minutes of sitting first thing in the morning. I sit on my yoga pad cross-legged, shut my eyes and I breathe. Those ten minutes is the perfect time to 'check in' with my being and ask, am I feeling happy or sad, uptight or relaxed. Then wait for the answers. They do come.

I do pranayama three times a week for one hour. I lie down and put my feet up on a wall and let my body relax. Anytime your legs are above your heart it lowers your heart rate, and when you lower your heart rate you automatically slow down and relax.

I am absolutely convinced that meditation will help you feel more together in this busy world we live in.

It is important to let go of all expectations when you are learning to meditate. Just be happy for where ever you are and do not give up. The reward is a quieter mind.

I highly recommend that you take the time to let yourself learn to meditate and then treasure it. It is a gift to you and one that can help you beyond words. The breathing works even in the most manic state. It has amazed me through the years how just taking ten deep breathes can help calm you and help you think more clearly.

The more tools you can find to ease your busy mind, the happier and more enjoyable your life will be. I encourage you to try meditation and give it your all.

There is thousands of great cd's in meditation. Have fun finding the right ones for you.

Exercize

When you are Bipolar, you live with unrest, anxiety, and impatience; you often feel like you could explode. There is an abundance of energy you do not know what to do with. The more manic, the more you feel like you could explode.

You must find an outlet, and exercise is a fabulous one, and a must. It is essential to your being to do exercise. When you are manic, you can work some of the energy off with exercise. And when you are depressed it helps the blues.

Exercise has always been a big part of my life. I have always had an abundance of energy and have looked for different outlets through swimming, dancing, volleyball, walking, biking, etc. I have always been a swimmer and I am sure it helped me though the years by allowing me to use up some of my excess energy, and to work off frustration, unrest and anxiety. And the breathing involved in swimming is a form of meditation for me. I have always felt more balanced and calmer after swimming for 20 minutes to an hour. I regularly use swimming as one of my breathing exercises.

I also like biking as an exercise to work off my impatience, anxiety, and unrest. It helps calm me also. I recommend biking for 20 minutes and building up to an hour.

Walking also helps me with impatience and anxiety, and it helps ground me. The more grounded I am the less scattered. The less scattered I feel the less I experience the fear. The less fear I have the less manic I am.

I find walking also helps with my digestion. I have always had trouble with my stomach. When I am manic, I become uptight, and my digestion suffers. A 20 minute to an hour walk "softens" my belly and calms me. Besides that I love walking because it gives me a chance to smell the flowers.

All types of exercises help to balance my energies. By balancing my energies I have a better chance of not going into a mood swing. My mood swings today are like night and day compared to what they were in my 20s and 30s.

Almost always, any kind of exercise can put a smile on my face. It is a proven fact that exercise stimulates endorphins, and makes you happier. Think of it as your work. The sooner you start doing it, the happier you will be.

I have learned through the years that it is necessary to do some form of exercise no matter how I am feeling. Still I know how much better I will feel if I exercise, so I know if I want to feel better, I must exercise, so I 'just do it'.

Exercise is a must. The best part is I always feel better. It is very easy to exercise when I am manic. But when I am depressed however, I feel it is important to share with you that it is hard to get started.

So do it. Find some things you enjoy and make it a part of your life.

Allowing Time

When you are Bipolar time can be your enemy, because you have the tendency to go in too many directions at once. Because your mind goes all the time, you tend to jump from one thing to another. You set goals that you could never hope to accomplish. The more you try to accomplish, the more frantic and frustrated you become. So adding extra time, in your plans is a must.

Allowing extra time in your plans sounds so easy; however in your plans, if you are manic, you typically have many more things planed to do than you would ever have enough time to accomplish.

Learning time management took me awhile to master, but once I did, it made a big difference in my stress level. Something as simple as adding an extra 15 minutes into your plans can make for a much happier day.

I have also learned to plan things ahead of time, and stick with the plan as best I can. I do not add more things to the plan once it is made.

I plan my week on Mondays. I realize when I make the plan that unforeseen things will come up during the week. Still, I do my best to stick with the plan. I try not to make big demands on myself, and then when other things come up, I do not become overwhelmed.

I become overwhelmed easily. If I have too much on my plate, I become scared, sometimes even terrified. It feels like something very bad is about to happen.

Here are some specific time management techniques that work for me:

1. I leave for an appointment 15 minutes early. (For the first 35 years of my life I was always 5 to 15 minutes late. This would cause me to become very manic. I felt lots of tension. There was a lot of unnecessary screaming, frustration and stress). That extra 15 minutes makes all the difference in the world; and is something that is easy to do.

2. I plan my week in advance. I have learned that I stay much calmer if I do not overload my schedule. I take time planning what I need to do each day. For me I know that I do not do well if I make more than two or three stops on a shopping day so I no longer try to do more than that. If I do, the result is always the same—I become very manic and impatient. It is not worth that trauma to my body mind and spirit to overload my schedule. It does not matter what other people can or can not do; we need to learn to honor ourselves and our needs.

3. I prepare for my day ahead of time. For example I lay out my clothes the night before. I have my coffee and juice ready to go. I make sure my purse and keys are together and I locate any paperwork or other things I might need.

4. I do my best not to procrastinate. This eliminates a lot of stress. If a letter needs to be mailed, I do not leave it sitting on a counter. If bills need to be paid, I pay them on time or ahead of time. I return phone

calls and emails in a timely manner. You will find that once you get in the habit of not procrastinating, you have extra time and less anxiety. It is great!

Allowing for an extra 15 minutes, not leaving things to the last moment, and not procrastinating will help to eliminate:

1. FEAR
2. ANXIETY
3. THE FEELING THAT SOMETHING BAD IS GOING TO HAPPEN
4. STRESS
5. ANGER
6. RAGE

Start small. For example; find a special place that you will always place your keys. That alone could save you 15 minutes each time you need your keys and eliminate much frustration.

Allowing more time is one of the many things you can do to help yourself. It can be done fairly easily, so make that commitment to yourself to allow more time in your schedule. And stick to it. It will make for a happier you.

ORGANIZATION

Part of being bipolar is a very busy mind. It is easy to get scattered. The more scattered I am, the more manic I am. When I become manic, I become overwhelmed easier. When I started taking lithium, it became much easier to be organized. It slowed my mind down enough to take the time to have things more together.

Being organized took some getting used to. I resisted it for years because my mind was too speedy, I did not want to stop long enough to put things in order.

Today it is so nice to walk out the door and know where important things are such as my keys, or my purse. Being organized helps me stay a lot calmer. Before lithium, I was always a nervous wreck by the time I left my house. I never knew where anything was, it always caused me to run late, and I hated it. I would be screaming and yelling at everyone like a crazy lady. It would take me some time to calm down. Not today. It feels so much better being organized—for me and for those that are around me.

I have learned to keep things in the same place.

1. KEYS
2. PHONES
3. PURSE

4.   ETC.

Organizing your time can save so much time. That was something I liked learning. Here are some tips:

Organize your time so you are always 15 minutes early. You don't put yourself under pressure of any kind when you leave the house and you start the day off on a better note by allowing that extra 15 minutes.

Do not leave things until the last minute.

Leaving things to the last minute always causes me to be anxious, frustrated and scattered. It is just not worth the anxiousness I create by being late.

Lay out your clothes the night before, along with whatever else you need the next day. This way you avoid any frustration when you can't find your shoes or purse, or something else that is important to you.

Being organized eliminates a lot of stress, and stress is the enemy. Look for anything you can do in your life to eliminate the stress. Organization is surely one if those things.

Commitments

Commitments put me in touch with my honor. They help me to be more responsible. For the first 35 years of my life, I did not do well with taking responsibility for my actions. Because of the Bipolar my thinking was very bizarre. My reasoning was poor. The healthier I became, the more responsible I became. Making commitments helps me stay responsible.

I write my commitments down. I give them a date and a time. I sign my commitments as though they were legal document. It is my word to me and I honor that. It helps me appreciate who I am. It helps me stay true to my being. I make commitments with my diet, exercise, meditations and many other things.

For example, I will write out that I choose to be off all sugars for the next 4 days. Then I date it, and sign it. My commitments can be for a month or a day. It does not matter the length of time; what matters is I honor my word. It is very powerful for me and rewarding. I may make a commitment to do 2 hours a day of exercise form 7 to 9 am for the month of Jan., then I date it and sign it. I may make a commitment to have no wine for a week and I date and sign it. Commitments help to keep me on track to my needs, and to stay a functional person.

Woke up this morning
what did I feel
spec spec spec so
much static

Then to Palenque
& I find that I
am spinning to a stop
Thanks !!!

CHOICES

"Your Choices Create Your Life".

Make positive choices with friends. How we choose our friends is very important. The first thing I look for in friends is how comfortable I feel in their presence. Do I leave them feeling less about myself or better. If I am around someone several different times and I leave them with a feeling that I have done something wrong or that they are not being honest with me, I stop seeing those people. There are always times that those feeling come up, but if they resurface all the time with someone, I move on. I look for people I have things in common with, and that are generous and kind. I am pretty much a loner, but I really enjoy a great conversation. I love to debate things. I enjoy one-on-one relationship rather than big gatherings. If there are more than 6 people, it feels too hectic for me. I used to love big crowds, when I was Manic all the time, but not anymore. Quiet dinners are my cup of tea now. I love feeling calm. It was a long time coming and anyone that helps me feel calm is a friend of mine. When I find myself in an uncomfortable situation, I leave. There was a time when I stayed in situations thinking I could make them better, ok, or more comfortable but not any more. That's because those situations can trigger the Manic or the Depression and it is one of the red flags I look for. Make the choice to stay away from people and things that irritate you. Bad situations can cause Manic or Depressions.

Honesty is another big one for me. I have to have it in a friendship. I feel very blessed to have the friends I have. I value those friendships with all my heart.

Moving to Mexico, (although I did not know it at the time) was a choice to start to slow down my life. Slowing my life down has made my life much calmer. When you are Bipolar, those calm days are true blessings.

Money has always been one of my issues, as it is with millions of other people. I have always been great at making money, but my management could have used some help.

It is important to have someone you trust help you with money situations. Money can be a problem if you are really manic. You might find yourself spending money you do not have, or charging up your credit cards. If you're on the depressive side that is dangerous also, because you just do not care.

I lost a million dollars in property when I was 38 because I loaned money without collateral; this was very bad and costly mistake. I was very Manic for several years before I lost my money. Because I was so manic, I had a lot of loose ends. I had too many things going on and little or no down time. I lost everything I owned 2 years after I was diagnosed Bipolar. My mind was going a mile a minute and I was working on getting a better handle on my life and I was not doing well at all. It took time to learn what I needed to change and to understand it well.

Had I had a financial advisor in those days, things would have been so much smoother. It is important to have someone set you on a good workable financial track. It could be your sister or a good friend-someone that can help you make a good plan for you. Your plan can be as simple as paying all your credit cards on the same day, to avoid forgetting to pay one. Or, it can be never letting your checking account go lower than $100.00. It needs to be a plan that keeps you on track and helps you to not get behind on any bills. I had so much anxiety about being late for a credit card payment, or not having enough money in the bank, that I literally could not think straight. Now my husband does most of the paper work and I have learned so much from him. It is so much easier to do paper work today because I have learned ways to slow my thinking down. Any kind of stress over money can trigger the Bipolar for me. The more things we can do to keep ourselves from stressing, the easier our life becomes. It is our choices that help us have a more functional life.

I have found through the years of my work with Bipolar, that your choice of work is very important. I had restaurants, beauty salons, and real estate, designed swimwear and held fashion shows. I worked 10 and 12 hour days, six days a week. I excelled in all of my careers; however they were much too hectic for me. I was in my 50s when I realized the difference a low key job could make on my being. Teaching yoga was that for me. The breathing, the wonderful breath, has made my life so much happier. I look for work now that keeps me relaxed.

When writing this book, I allow myself 2 to 3 hours a day. I do not keep going when I feel myself getting uptight. That is new for me. I am glad that with each New Year, there is another new discovery that helps me with the Bipolar. The less uptight I am the better I can control the manic.

Family never really will understand the Bipolar, unless they were also are bipolar. When I first found out I was Bipolar, no one in my family would talk to me about it. They all whispered behind my back. I hated it. I just wanted someone to sit down and talk to me, but it never happened. I made a choice to stop talking about the condition because it always seemed to upset people. My sister and cousins were the only ones I talked with it about it. I asked my sister to monitor me a few times a week by talking to me on the phone or stopping by and letting me know if I was sounding more relaxed, or manic. We would talk every few days or so. And that helped me when I started taking lithium in terms of understanding how the drug affected me.

Both my mother and father died without ever having a discussion with me about my illness. All my life they pretended that everything was ok. When I attempted suicides, it was never talked about either. I guess it scared them: it sure did me.

Diet is one of the most important choices of being a healthy Bipolar person. My cousin Joni taught me a lot. She knows today more than any nutritionist with which I have worked. The first thing she did was taking me off of all sugar and starts a detoxifying program with me. When I began working with her, I was in the depths of depression. I had lost all my property, was broke, was having problems with my daughters, and was refusing to take that last piece of responsibility for my life. The depression was so severe I tried to kill myself by taking a bottle of lithium. That was my last time I ever made that choice in my life. It was the beginning of really becoming healthy. I worked with all the discipline I could muster up, and a year later, I was happier and stronger than I had ever been. And the depression was gone. I worked for several more years with a few nutritionists and learned the best things for my body to eat, to stay healthy and to be strong. Limiting my sugar is one of the best things I have learned to do to help my body. My choice to eat healthy was a big one for me and more powerful than I could have imagined. My slogan for years has been HEALTH IS WEALTH, and I believe that with all my heart.

It is wise to make the choice to exercise regularly. It is another great tool, and can help you in many ways. I walk, swim, bike ride, do yoga, and dance. I need strong exercise to let go of some of the tension and rage I carry in my being. Swimming, biking and dancing is good for working out anxiety and frustrations. I find that walking for 20 minutes to an hour nice and brisk helps my digestion. Yoga calms me down and just makes me happier. I marvel at the effects yoga has for me and the Bipolar. It allows me to slow down to breathe. And the breath is so calming. Find out what your body needs. Experiment with different type of exercise and make your choice as to what helps you the most. The more involved you are in your recovery, the better for you and those that love you.

Being positive just feels better. It is ok to feel every emotion. Focus on all you do have and say thank you for your blessings. They are there.

Say thank you100 times a day, everyday, for all the things you do have. It works; things get better the more you say thank you. Try it for a week and watch what happens. It is your choice.

I find it is a good choice for me to have more alone time than most. Having that extra space is very calming. The calmer I am the more relaxed I become; the more relaxed the less manic.

Find those things that can help you love yourself more; make the choice to be on your side.

Sleep

My sleep pattern is a key indicator for knowing when a cycle is starting. When you are bipolar, your mind is like a wave. It goes up into the manic and down into the depression. The more present you are with the wave, the easier it is for you to know what is about to start or what has already started. I can keep the manic from going too strong if I can catch it at a certain point. The morning writing keeps me in touch with the wave. If I do not catch the cycle in time, my sleep can be off for a few days or weeks.

I have never been a perfect sleeper. For years I believed that that was the case for most people.

My insomnia started when I was in grade school. I would be up until 2 or 3 in the morning, and then tired in school. After days of not sleeping, my temper and my impatience were stretched. It was very difficult at times for my friends because I was often out of control due to the lack of sleep and being manic. With yoga and meditation my sleeping pattern has improved a great deal. The breath work in yoga and meditation is very important in calming my mind and body to help me to sleep. The difference the yoga, and the meditation makes is truly amazing. It can work as good as any tranquilizers with no negative side effects.

I find that lying down with my feet up on a wall in the middle of the day for 20 minutes to an hour has a calming effect on my being. The calmer I am, the better I sleep. The breathing also relieves the tensions from the day, and helps so much with my impatience.

Eating dinner between 4 and 6 also helps my sleeping pattern. My body isn't trying to digest a late meal. It can concentrate better on my relaxation.

I am a light sleeper. Lights turning on or different noises can keep me from sleeping, so it is important to have a quiet room when I retire.

Diet plays a huge part in my sleeping. Sugar is the enemy—I cannot stress that enough. My manic swings are much less intense and I sleep much better when I am watching my sugar intake. Also, I make sure to have no caffeine after 2 in the afternoon.

Procrastination also plays havoc on my sleeping. It is very important to take care of things and not wait a day or two, or put things on the back burner for some time. That only causes stress and stress triggers the manic. The simpler I keep things, the less confusion I experience. Confusion triggers the manic, and the manic causes sleeping problems. When I become stressful, my sleeping patter becomes off which causes me to be even more impatient. To avoid the stress, I avoid the procrastination.

When sleep is missed for days, it is very difficult to function properly. I become scattered, confused and fearful. It is not a comfortable place to be.

I work with the 14 things on my list daily, and all of them help me with my sleeping pattern.

A few days a month I have insomnia now, not daily. Normally around the full moon I have a hard time with sleeping. Being able to sleep better has helped me in a hundred different ways. I am very grateful that I have found the tools to aid my sleeping. You can too.

Art

My first real involvement with art was after a Primal Workshop (working with child-hood core issues). It was a very intense workshop and a lot of feelings were stirred up. The lady leading the workshop put out a lot of different sizes of paper, chalks, watercolors, oils, and paint brushes. She instructed us to paint or draw what we were feeling. When I started painting, it gave me a sense of emptying my soul. My painting was very busy, like my mind so it put me in touch with my busy mind in a different way.

I loved painting. I felt a great release from painting in that first experience, and 20 years later, I still get a release and a much better sense of how I am doing emotionally.

I have learned to watch my choice of color because it helps me to understand my feelings better. There are times my mind is so busy that all of the emotions I am feeling get too cluttered for me to see clearly. My choice of colors when I paint shows me what I am feeling.

FOR INSTANCE, for me,
ORANGE IS PAIN
GREEN IS HEALTH
BROWN IS SADNESS
PINK IS LOVE

RED IS RAGE
BLACK IS ANGER

Looking at the colors I choose when I paint is one of the ways I keep in touch my subconscious. I do not always catch the mood swings in my conscious mind but my subconscious does.

My paintings also help me to judge where I am in the bipolar wave. If I start to see a lot more red or black in my paintings, I know I am becoming more manic. If my colors are soft, I know I am in a more centered place. When I start seeing a lot of browns and oranges, it is a red flag that I am more depressed.

When my art is very busy, I know I am becoming more manic. How busy my art is tells me how busy my mind is. My mind is going really fast when my paintings become busy. Interestingly my best art is always when I am manic. Often I draw in ink or pencil without colors. Normally, at these times, I tend to be more on the manic side, and it shows in the busy-ness of the drawings.

Besides using painting to help me be in touch with my feelings I also find it to be very relaxing and calming. It helps quiet my mind and, in doing so, helps control the intensity of mood swings. It is a nice way for me to empty out some of the clutter in my mind and being. When I feel less clutter, I feel less fear.

Art is very relaxing and calming. It will calm me and helps quiet my mind. So when I paint a lot happens for me: I become calmer and I can relate better to where I am on the "wave" by my choice of colors and by the busy-ness of my painting.

Here are some things I have done. I do not consider myself an Artist. The art I do is to stay in touch with my feelings and emotions. The more in touch with my feelings and emotions the easier the mood swings. I suggest you try this too to see how it works for you.

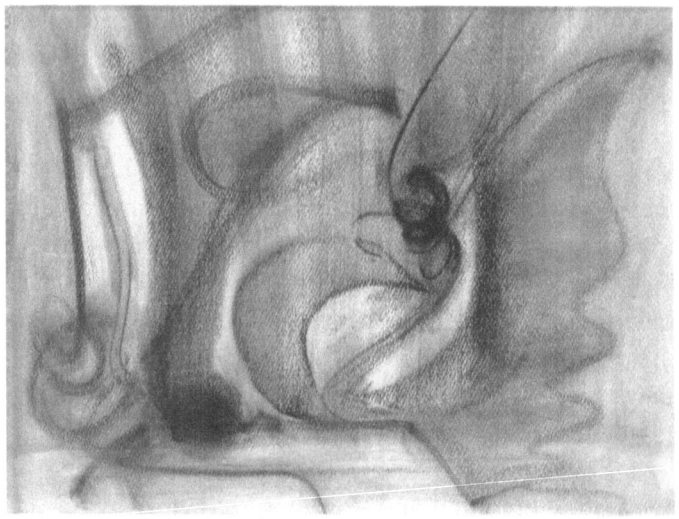

then the joy
can return
my sadness will
subside
The peace will
come

know I am safe
Help me to see the
beauty in all & open
more to compassion
& avoid the feeling
of judgement I love
you June

Giving Service

Giving service is a wonderful way to say thank you to the universe. We all have so much to be thankful for. Start off doing a service without any intension of getting something for it. You could teach, or work with children or animals. You can every minute of everyday express openness and love to all things. You can find ways to help those less fortunate than you. A simple thing, but one that is really appreciated, is to be present when someone is talking to you. We all want to feel important and cared about. Work hard to stay away from all judgment. Be part of the solution and not part of the problem.

Giving service helps to make our life bigger, and our world a better place to be in. Give service from the heart. What we give freely comes back in so many wonderful ways.

Do not get caught up in comparing what you do and what is done for you. The universe has a great way of balancing things for us.

How To Use Tools

I have given you many different ways to succeed in life with a bipolar condition. But where do you start? First thing; make a list of the areas you want to improve in your behavior and gain control over. For me, one of those areas was having more patience. My lack of patience has caused me a lot of problems through the years.

Next choose two things on the list that you want to do to improve the areas of your behavior you listed. (For example "begin a walking program", "change my diet"). Do not try to do more at the beginning. Set reasonable goals. You might want someone to help you with your goals and the behaviors you choose to work on.

Work on the two goals that you choose for a week. Every day check in with yourself and see how you feel about working with the things you have chosen to work with, then grade them from one to ten with ten being the highest score grade. At the end of a week, review your scores and put the one with the most points on a separate list.

The following week pick two more goals, and do the same thing: grade them daily, and pick the one that has the most points, at the end of the week, and put it on a separate list. After you have worked with all your goals, choose the ones that were the most help for you. It could be two of them, or all of them.

So let's say out of all your goals the highest scored were, exercise and diet. Start doing them regularly. When you feel you have integrated them into your life style, pick another with the next highest points, and then another, until you have worked all on your list.

Think of yourself as if you are in kindergarten, learning daily a new way to work with your life. Changing your diet alone could take a year to do properly. However with each new step, you are closer to having a more functional life. The more tools you integrated, the more functional your life will be and the easier and happier you will be.

As in kindergarten, you are learning a lot of new things and many may need some guidance. For example, if you are working with your diet, you will probably want to find a good nutritionist and work closely with him or her. A good nutritionist can help you find the diet that will help your body work its best. For me getting off sugar has changed my manic mood swings in ways I would never have thought possible. So often I speak with Bipolar individuals about their sugar intake, and they have no desire to make any changes. They do not believe it will make a difference. I had to get very sick before I would go off sugar myself. If you just start with eliminating all sugars from your diet for a month, you would most likely notice a big change in your sleeping patterns, your patience, and your energy level. My experience with sugar is that it is the ENEMY. It makes my mood swings much more intense, and plays havoc with my patience. I found keeping a journal on my progress was a great help and something I could look back on and study.

If your goal is to start exercise start slow. Start with 15 minutes and work up to an hour. Set a certain time each day to exercise and stick to your time frame. Make a commitment to yourself to do this. It is a great accomplishment to take good care of you, and the commitments help us keep to our goals.

If your goal is to do art, do the same things pick a time, stick to it, and start making a commitment to yourself to continue. Art takes a variety of foams—arranging flowers, cooking, painting, clay, working with designing cloth, gardening, and much more. Art can be a way of (emptying your holdings) so you will feel calmer and happier. I find that after I do any type of art that I am calmer and less scattered.

The 2nd week you pick 2 new things. The 2nd week you might pick yoga and meditation. Begin with writing down your commitment to do yoga and meditation for the week, date it and sign, but most important honor it. Make your commitment as to what time you can do the yoga and meditation and organize your day. I find that if I do my yoga 1st thing in the morning it works best for me. It is easy to do a little meditation when you are doing your yoga. In the morning I do my yoga practice with about 10 minutes of meditation at the end. I like to do another meditation in the late afternoon also. It helps to calm me after a days work.

At the end of the day, grade what you are doing. Let's say you are really enjoying the yoga and mediation a lot and do not want to start anything new for a few weeks, and just stay with your choices of yoga, and meditation. Stay with the two. And work with getting a good pattern going. They say if you do something for a month it becomes a habit. But let's say you want to try 2 new things instead, and you choose morning writings, and organization.

If your goal is morning writing, I suggest that you write as soon as you awaken. Just start writing and empty out all in your busy mind and air your frustrations. Do not read anything until a week or so and then look for some kind of pattern to what you are writing. Maybe you talk about not sleeping well, or wanting to slow down, look for something to appear in your writings, some kind of pattern. In a short period of time, you will be able to see what you need to work on more or pay better attention to.

Organization is a foreign word to most people who are Bipolar. I used to have a boss that would go to my messy desk and put everything on it into a box. It was so painful for me at that time to take things out of the box 1 by1 and organize them. Lithium really helped me slow down enough to start to reorganize my life. Start small. Try just leaving your keys in the same spot for a week. Do not set your goals too high. Don't start to reorganize your whole house; you will fail. Take things slow. Watch how things help or hinder you. At the end of this week, do the same things as in the previous week—grade what you've chosen as your goals, take one off the list, and add a few more for the next week.

It is important to thank yourself for all that you are beginning to do. It is important to appreciate that you are nurturing yourself. It is important not to bite off more than you can chew. If you set your goals smaller and a achieve them, you will start to appreciate yourself in a new way.

The more time you put into helping yourself, the easier your life will become. It will not always be easy or fun, but it will be rewarding to re—learn things that will help you succeed with being bipolar.

As the time goes by, you will understand in a more functional way what is needed for your mind, body and spirit. It will take time. It will be difficult, but so worth the effort. Everything you learn about your needs leads to more and more happiness in your world.

In time, the hope is you will find the tools to help you, and you will most likely start adding more tools to your list. Remember our minds are our only limitations to what can and can't be done.

Have fun getting to re-know you. And say thank you all the time for all that is there for you.

Work Book

The Goal of the Work Book is to help you to have a more manageable, functional life.

1. Using the Tools.
   A. Pick 2 items from the list below:

   1. Check in Person
   2. Morning Writings
   3. Diet
   4. Yoga
   5. Meditation
   6. Exercise
   7. Allowing Time
   8. Organization
   9. Choices
   10. Commitments
   11. Sleep
   12. Art
   13. Giving Service
   14. Being with Nature

B. Set Goals

    1. Take the two items and decide where you want to do them and how much time you will spend.

C. Make a commitment of your goals and write them down.

    2. Sample: I commit to 30 minutes of Art a day in my living room, and doing yoga on the beach for 20 minutes, for the next 7 days. Starting on, Jan.2, 2010 to Jan 8th 2010. And sign it.

D. Work the two items you choose for one week.

E. Grade the items you have chosen on how well you like doing them and if you are finding them helpful. Grade them from 1 to 10 (10 being the highest).

F. At the end of the week place your scores on the "weeks highest score column".

G. Week two pick two more and do the same each week until you complete the 14 items on the list. When you complete the list pick the 2 highest scores and start making them a part your daily life.

H. You can add more to your list at anytime. Feel free to intergrades your personal choices into the list. Be sure to write down your commitments each time.

J. Every month check on your progress. Be proud of what you accomplished. With each month you will begin to see some changes. Be grateful for them, big or small. The change is not overnight, but all the discipline is well rewarded, in a happier life. Enjoy becoming a healthier, happier person.

SAMPLE

WORKBOOK

DAILY SCORE			
DAY	YOGA	MORNING WRITTINGS	HIGHEST WEEKLY SCORE
Monday	5	7	49
Tuesday	5	7	
Wednesday	5	7	
Thrusday	5	7	
Friday	5	7	
Saturday	5	7	
Sunday	5	7	
TOTAL	35	49	

WORKBOOK

DAILY SCORE			
DAY	ART	DIET	HIGHEST WEEKLY SCORE
Monday	4	6	42
Tuesday	4	6	
Wednesday	4	6	
Thrusday	4	6	
Friday	4	6	
Saturday	4	6	
Sunday	4	6	
TOTAL	28	42	

WORKBOOK

DAILY SCORE			
DAY	YOGA	MORNING WRITTINGS	HIGHEST WEEKLY SCORE
Monday			
Tuesday			
Wednesday			
Thrusday			
Friday			
Saturday			
Sunday			
TOTAL			

WORKBOOK

DAILY SCORE			
DAY	ART	DIET	HIGHEST WEEKLY SCORE
Monday			
Tuesday			
Wednesday			
Thrusday			
Friday			
Saturday			
Sunday			
TOTAL			

WORKBOOK

DAILY SCORE			
DAY	YOGA	MORNING WRITTINGS	HIGHEST WEEKLY SCORE
Monday			
Tuesday			
Wednesday			
Thrusday			
Friday			
Saturday			
Sunday			
TOTAL			

WORKBOOK

DAILY SCORE			
DAY	ART	DIET	HIGHEST WEEKLY SCORE
Monday			
Tuesday			
Wednesday			
Thrusday			
Friday			
Saturday			
Sunday			
TOTAL			

WORKBOOK

DAILY SCORE			
DAY	YOGA	MORNING WRITTINGS	HIGHEST WEEKLY SCORE
Monday			
Tuesday			
Wednesday			
Thrusday			
Friday			
Saturday			
Sunday			
TOTAL			

WORKBOOK

DAILY SCORE			
DAY	ART	DIET	HIGHEST WEEKLY SCORE
Monday			
Tuesday			
Wednesday			
Thrusday			
Friday			
Saturday			
Sunday			
TOTAL			

WORKBOOK

DAILY SCORE			
DAY	YOGA	MORNING WRITTINGS	HIGHEST WEEKLY SCORE
Monday			
Tuesday			
Wednesday			
Thrusday			
Friday			
Saturday			
Sunday			
TOTAL			

WORKBOOK

DAILY SCORE			
DAY	ART	DIET	HIGHEST WEEKLY SCORE
Monday			
Tuesday			
Wednesday			
Thrusday			
Friday			
Saturday			
Sunday			
TOTAL			

WORKBOOK

DAILY SCORE			
DAY	YOGA	MORNING WRITTINGS	HIGHEST WEEKLY SCORE
Monday			
Tuesday			
Wednesday			
Thrusday			
Friday			
Saturday			
Sunday			
TOTAL			

WORKBOOK

DAILY SCORE			
DAY	ART	DIET	HIGHEST WEEKLY SCORE
Monday			
Tuesday			
Wednesday			
Thrusday			
Friday			
Saturday			
Sunday			
TOTAL